30 Days to a Raise

30 Days to a Raise

a Raise

**EARN WHAT YOU ARE WORTH IN
THIRTY STRATEGIC STEPS!**

Employee Edition

Jeff Marcu

ISBN: 1983755419
ISBN-13: 9781983755415

Contents

Introduction

The biggest complaint I hear from people in the work-force is that they don't believe they are getting paid what they are worth. Some of them are right, while others are actually getting paid pretty close to their value.

I have noticed that many people like to blame their employers for paying wages that are lower than acceptable. That's something that always baffles me! Why is it your employer's job to pay you what you are worth? Your boss is not responsible for making sure you earn a fair wage. You are. Sure, an employer should treat its staff fairly, but ultimately, you live in a free market where you ultimately determine your fate and your earning power.

The purpose of this book is to show you how to start earning more money and feel like you are highly compensated in comparison to your value in the marketplace.

I will show you practical steps that can help you earn more and have a more fulfilling career. This simple step-by-step guide can increase your value by helping you lay the ground-work for accomplishing these goals within thirty days.

There are many factors to earning more money and changing the trajectory of your career, so you must under-stand that there are no guarantees that you will get a raise after reading this book. But I suspect that you will definitely increase your chances of earning more money if you apply the concepts that you think could work for you.

There is one very important thing to remember as you start to understand who you are and how you will earn more money: be honest with yourself. Assess your work, output, and role in your workplace objectively. If you owned the com-pany where you work, would you like the current you as one of your employees? Some people are in denial about why they are not earning more money. They like to blame other people for their place in life. Once you stop doing that and take steps to increase your value in the workplace, you will quickly realize that you are worth more than you are currently making, and people will want to pay you that value once you demonstrate that you are worth it.

You might be wondering how I am qualified to coach you to get a raise. This is what I do for a living. As the CEO of a successful broadcast talent firm, I create outrageously successful and lucrative careers and lives for my clients that wildly exceed their imaginations. The powerful steps I share in this book are the same techniques I teach my clients. I have doubled, tripled, and even quadrupled my clients' salaries. I have completely transformed who they are and what they do—all this in an ultracompetitive industry. You can do the same in your career and life. We all can if we know the steps that create change and how to execute them.

Before we get started, let me share a bit about my writing style and how I develop my books. I have developed a *30 Days* series of books that are easy to read, describing concepts that are simple to apply and actually work. I strive to write books that are actionable and impactful. I have *tried* to read many "motivational" books that were so complex that I lost interest before I was able to finish them. With my books, I hope that you can read one concept per day, work to apply each one, and finish them in thirty days.

I will guide you through this book by asking you questions along the way. For each concept, I label these as **key questions that will inspire you to take action and create change.** Answering them will help you better understand specifically what you need to do to create real change. They are very basic and will quickly help you understand why you might be experiencing challenges in earning what you are worth. I have left room for you to write your answers after each question, or you can keep a separate journal. Writing down your answers will hold you more accountable to your goals than just thinking about them.

There is nothing I describe in this book that is beyond common sense. My goal is to motivate you to take the steps that will help you reach your true and unlimited potential. Are you ready to start earning more money? Let's begin!

CHAPTER 1

Your first ninety days at work could be
the most important.

Your first ninety days in a new position may set the tone
for the rest of your career with that company. During
those first three months, your management and coworkers
form opinions about you and your work ethic. First impres-
sions count, and they last. It is sometimes very difficult to
change those opinions if people have already decided that
they know who you are.

In a new position, you want to do everything you can to
stand out and show you are a leader and a hard worker with
a positive attitude. This is the ninety-day quick-start program
that I share with my clients who begin new positions. It's very
simple: work hard, have a positive attitude, volunteer to contribute extra when the situation warrants it, and do what your

employer is paying you to do. That's it. Be the employee you would want if you were the boss. When you establish this reputation from the start, you have a better chance of management viewing you as someone who is promotable and deserves a raise.

A manager wants to know he or she has made the right decision in hiring you. It is your responsibility to prove him or her right.

Key questions that will inspire you to take action and create change:

1) What specific steps can you take during the first ninety days at your new position that will show you are a standout team member?

2) What can you offer that is unique and valuable to your employer?

3) What can you contribute that is extra and beyond the expectations of your role?

4)   What negative attributes do you want to avoid? For example, "I will not get involved in work rumors and earn a reputation as a gossip."

It is important to work hard during your entire employment, but it is essential that you have a strong start in proving who you are. You will find the rest of your employment at this company more beneficial to you and increase your chances of getting promotions and raises if you establish yourself as a valuable resource in the first ninety days.

CHAPTER 2

Find out what your employer wants and needs.

There is absolutely nothing wrong with asking how to excel. I always suggest that my clients ask prospective or current employers what the superstar at the company does to be a star. Asking for guidance is the easiest way for you to know the key areas where you should focus. Once you learn how your employer defines "superstar," you can start to strategize how you can align your work with that definition.

Be sure to ask detailed questions. You want more than the answer that the star of the company works hard. You need to understand what about that hard work is meaningful to your employer. You should also get an understanding of the personal traits the manager likes in team members. Does he or she like independent workers? People who collaborate? What else?

Key questions that will inspire you to take action and create change:

1) How can you add your personal touch to the list of items that are important to your employer? Once you figure out what it takes to excel, think about how you can add your own personality and approach to stand out and make a difference.

2) After you learn who the leaders in your workplace are, observe how they work. From your observations, what makes them different from everyone else?

3) Are there themes or patterns you noticed in the answers your employer gave you about what the superstars do at work? Try to look past the answers and determine the patterns of behavior that your employer appreciates. Develop your own list of what you will do to be a leader based on that information.

Once you have an understanding of what the superstar does at your company, you have the tools to be the next star. If you asked your employer the right questions, you now have your blueprint for success. While a checklist of what you need to do is a great starting point, proper execution of that list is key to your success. When you gain a good understanding of the culture of your workplace, you will know how to best execute your strategy in a positive and productive way.

CHAPTER 3

If possible and legal, stop tracking your hours.

So many employer-employee relationships become strained in the battle over one of the most important resources we have—time. Generally, employers want more of our time, but employees may not always want to devote so much of it to a career. This can be one of the biggest conflicts between employers and employees.

While I respect a balance between work and personal life, I think there are ways to pursue your personal life while working hard and advancing your career.

If possible, I advise you to stop tracking your hours. Of course, if you earn an hourly wage, legally, you must track them. But if you earn a salary and are not eligible for overtime, you may enjoy your career more and really have the chance to excel if you stop keeping a mental log of what your boss "owes" you because you put in some extra hours. I have found that many people build up resentment and want everything to be 100 percent fair. Unfortunately, most of the time, you will find that not everything at work is fair.

Once you start looking at the bigger picture, you may realize that your focus should be not on your extra hour or two here or there but instead on how you are building your image, value, and worth by showing that you are not keeping track of every little extra thing you do.

Key questions that will inspire you to take action and create change:

1) Are you keeping a mental or physical list of everything extra you are doing at work? You may want to consider ending that practice. As your list grows, so will your resentment. You can maintain a general log of your major accomplishments to reference in performance reviews to demonstrate what you have contributed.

2) If you owned the company, would you still be tracking your hours? Probably not. Be the team member you would want to hire.

3) Do you have a long-term plan to benefit from your extra efforts? Understand why it is valuable and worthwhile for you to stop counting hours and start contributing.

4) Do you realize the difference between not tracking your hours and having an employer that simply takes advantage of you? It is important to identify the difference between being generous with your time and a company taking advantage of it.

When I look back on my career, I had positions where I did not track my hours, and it paid off with promotions and raises. I gladly devoted more time to my career and my employer's goals and efforts because I knew I was investing in myself.

However, I had one position where there was no long-term payoff for working extra, and management generally expected significant amounts of extra work for no long-term reward. In these situations, the struggle between employer and employee usually grows, and the workplace culture shows the signs of a negative environment. If you find yourself in that situation, it may be time to reevaluate your career and consider whether staying with the company is beneficial for you. Are your employer's goals aligned with yours?

Not tracking your hours is a psychological tool you can use to prevent yourself from resenting your employer, but it should not stop you from determining whether your relationship with your employer is equitable.

CHAPTER 4

Work extra when needed.

Working extra when needed is a pretty straightforward concept, but you need to understand how to best use this to build your reputation and set yourself up for future raises and promotions.

Working extra is closely tied to the previous chapter of not tracking your hours. Not tracking your hours is more of a psychological tool you can use to prevent yourself from resenting your employer because you are maintaining a list or scorecard of how your relationship is not equitable.

You need to understand how your workplace operates and in what areas you can offer meaningful contributions. When I suggest you work extra when needed, I don't mean you should just mindlessly spend all your free time at work.

You need to offer your help strategically, at the times and in the places when you will make the most impact for your employer and for yourself.

Key questions that will inspire you to take action and create change:

1) In what ways can you contribute extra work that truly offers value to your employer?

2) By contributing extra at work, what is your long-term goal? Do you want to develop a reputation as a hard worker? Be eligible for future raises? Add to your knowledge base and build your résumé?

3) Are there times when your extra work can offer more value to your company? For example, are there busier times, when others will appreciate your extra work? At a tax firm, for example, tax season would be that time.

Working extra is a great way to show you are a contributing member of your team, but make sure you understand your limits and determine whether the payoff for working extra hours is there for you.

CHAPTER 5

Don't be predictable.

Most of us fall into routines at work that make us average. Habit breeds mediocrity. If your thoughts about work become predictable, your actions at work will become predictable as well. How can you earn a raise if you continue to do the same things over and over again?

Let me be specific about what I mean by "not being predictable." I am not asking you to try crazy things to stand out. I am simply asking you to get out of your routine and push yourself beyond average. If your actions result in a benefit to your company and your employer starts to notice that you are doing extraordinary things and getting extraordinary results, you are paving the way for your success.

Key questions that will inspire you to take action and create change:

1) What extra efforts can you make that will show you possess skills no one else does?

2) Can you measure your risk-to-reward ratio to determine whether your actions will benefit your employer and your overall career trajectory?

3) Are your actions generally acceptable workplace behavior? Positive unpredictability that yields positive results is excellent when it fits well within your workplace culture.

4) Can you find ways to constantly reinvent yourself and earn the reputation as an innovator who sparks impactful change?

If you can mold your image into that of someone who is not afraid to take calculated risks that can yield positive results, you will rise to the top of the line as someone who is promotable and worth the investment.

I think you will also find your role much more rewarding when you are able to innovate and create new opportunities for yourself and your company. When you establish yourself as someone who excels past average, that is exactly how people will view you. Take some risks, and leave the predictability to someone else.

CHAPTER 6

Don't be like all your coworkers. If you just do what everyone else does, why should you get a raise?

While it is important to understand what the superstars do at your workplace, it is equally important to understand how everyone else performs. Chances are that most people at work are either average or underperformers.

It can be very easy to get comfortable at work and become complacent because your coworkers are in that mind-set. Your odds of getting a raise significantly decrease if you (and your work) are just like everyone else.

I have found that mediocrity can be contagious at work. But just because others are not performing at their optimal level, that does not mean you shouldn't.

Your goal is to build a strategy that will help you stand out and show you are a candidate for advancement and a raise. Some people tell me that they think if they stand out from the crowd at work, their coworkers will resent them. That is absolute nonsense. When you work hard, you are not hurting anyone else. You are just helping yourself and your company. Everyone else has the same opportunity as you do to work hard and make a difference and a lasting impression. In most cases, you are not splitting your pay with your coworkers, so you should not be concerned with their output or how they perceive your hard work.

Key questions that will inspire you to take action and create change:

1) What are people doing in your workplace that makes them average?

2) What can you do differently to rise above the crowd of mediocrity?

3) In what ways does the culture in your workplace allow people to be average?

4) What can you do to change the culture at work?

You will quickly find out that it is pretty easy to stand out at work. You need to develop a strategy that works for you so you can be effective at your workplace. When you gain an understanding of the general culture there, you will quickly identify key areas where you can excel and start developing your reputation as someone who is a candidate for raises and promotions.

Remember, it is very easy and tempting to fall in line with the average group of people at work. I challenge you push past average and work hard to lead and not follow.

CHAPTER 7

Reassess your skills.

At the beginning of this book, I noted that people blame their employers when they are not getting raises or not getting paid what they are worth. I mentioned that I wanted you to be honest with yourself while you are reading this book.

So, let me ask you: Do your skills warrant a raise? Are you *really* worth more than what you earn? These may be tough questions for you to answer objectively. These key questions can help you figure out realistic and accurate answers.

Key questions that will inspire you to take action and create change:

1) Is your skill set above what your industry considers average, or do you possess the bare minimum of skills?

2) Have you added to your skills as you career has evolved?

3) Do your skills align with your company's objectives?

4) Are you keeping up with or exceeding industry expectations?

For you to create real change and a path to a more lucrative career, you need to gain a really honest understanding and assessment of your skills and of what you need to do to up your game. If you are in constant denial and only blame your boss for your current pay scale, then you will probably remain stuck in the vicious cycle of complaining, not changing, and never getting what you really want out of your career.

It is your obligation to figure out where you are lacking, where you can improve, and how to most effectively update your skills.

CHAPTER 8

Get more education.

One way to increase your value in the workplace is to get more education. What is the average level of education for your coworker, and what level of education do you have? What type of education do your bosses have? They may be your bosses for a reason.

Before you blindly start seeking additional degrees, you first have to understand whether education will really help you earn more money. There are careers where education is essential. Doctors, lawyers, and educators require certain types of education just to enter their fields. However, additional degrees will do you no good in some sales positions, for example, if you are not a good salesperson.

If education will add to your value in the workplace, it's important to evaluate what type of schooling is a worthwhile investment.

Key questions that will inspire you to take action and create change:

1) Is there a certain type of degree or education that will help you earn more money in your career?

2) What types of degrees or education are trending as important in your industry?

3) What are the future needs in your industry? Is there education you can pursue now that will put you on the cutting edge and significantly increase your value? If you have learned something that most people in your industry have not yet, your value should be higher than that of your peers.

4) Are you pursuing education that is outdated or not relevant in your field? All the education in the world will not help you get a raise if it is not relevant in your industry.

Since you are going to focus your education in a field that is beneficial and relevant in your industry, be sure to check whether your employer will pay for all or a portion of it. Sometimes there are strings attached to employer-sponsored education reimbursement, so make sure you understand any stipulations. Some arrangements may commit you to staying at your current employer for a certain amount of time if it pays for your education. That is not always a bad thing as long as you understand what you are agreeing to and are happy with the terms.

CHAPTER 9

Earn credentials and certifications.

In addition to traditional education, you can increase your earning power by acquiring relevant credentials and certifications. In fact, it may be quicker to gain these, thereby increasing your value sooner. You have to determine the value of any certification and make sure you are not wasting your time and money on bogus credentials.

Many evolving industries continually introduce new certification programs. Certifications are very prevalent, for example, in real estate. When the real-estate market crashes, the industry offers certifications for agents to become short-sale or foreclosure specialists. When there is a strong seller's market, the industry offers certifications for buyer's agents and negotiation experts who specialize in helping buyers find homes in competitive markets.

Find the credentials relevant to your industry, and capitalize on promoting yourself as an expert in your field.

Key questions that will inspire you to take action and create change:

1) Will having additional credentials make you more valuable and qualify for higher-paying positions?

2) What are the hottest certifications in your industry right now? What accreditation do you need to be in demand and relevant now?

3) What is the next generation of credentials in your industry? What accreditation do you need to be in demand and relevant in the future?

4) What type of expertise does your employer need? Ask your employer what type of expertise it needs in its organization now and in the future.

5) What types of certifications do the leaders in your industry have?

It is not just the credentials that will increase your value; you must also take care with how you apply your new expertise to your position. You can have a dozen certifications, but if you don't properly execute what you have learned, you will probably not see a raise anytime soon. Make sure you have a solid understanding of the subject you have learned and of how to demonstrate your expertise effectively to others.

CHAPTER 10

Question your role.

If you feel like you are not earning what you are worth, you should question your role at your workplace and look for reasons why you are not making the money you think you deserve.

By asking yourself questions, you can figure out why you are not making the kind of money you want. Your *role* refers to how you fit into your workplace and how your employers view you and your performance. Once you gain a better understanding of what you are and are not doing, you will understand how to make updates to create powerful change that will hopefully lead to increased compensation and opportunities.

Key questions that will inspire you to take action and create change:

1) How essential is your role in your workplace? Are you considered a necessary and vital part of your company's success?

2) If not, what can you do to make your role more important to your employer and more fulfilling to yourself?

3) Are you in the right position for your skill set?

4) Why do you work the way you do? It's a simple question, but you need to figure out if you are doing things at work out of habit or because they are effective and impactful.

After you figure out what your role is, it should be easy for you to identify what updates to make to what you do and how you offer value. In return, your employer should notice your evolution. If not, it is your responsibility to bring it to your employer's attention. In demonstrating how you have changed and why, you will be creating goodwill, proving your value and your willingness to make important updates that benefit your company.

CHAPTER 11

Be personable and likable at work.

You can master all the work credentials and have high output at work, but if you are not likable and do not have an engaging personality, your opportunities may be limited. In addition to promoting and giving raises based on work ethic and talent, it is human nature for employers to promote people based on whom they like.

Let's be sure to differentiate between your work personality and your personality outside of working hours. I am not suggesting that you bring your Friday-night-out-with-friends personality to the workplace. Instead, you need to understand your workplace culture and how your personality could contribute to that environment.

You may generally find that the people who are rewarded most at your company are those who are universally liked and with whom people find it easy to get along. This is not always the case, but oftentimes, those who know how to relate well with others reap the rewards of their efforts.

Key questions that will inspire you to take action and create change:

1) Do you have a good balance of work ethic and personality?

2) How do other people perceive you? You can easily ask your coworkers for a little feedback on that.

3) Are you making an effort to be kind and helpful to your coworkers and management?

4) Are you the type of person you would want to be around at work?

5) Is your mood consistent at work? When people approach you at work to talk, is your personality consistent? Even during your challenging days, are you likable?

I have discovered that some people find being personable at work a challenge. Sometimes it is because they are not happy with what they are doing. If you are in this situation, I encourage you to figure out what is making you unhappy and work to make changes. If you become the person everyone else likes and appreciates, your opportunities will consistently grow.

CHAPTER 12

Get to know your management, and let them know you.

In the previous chapter, I challenged you to be personable and likable. Now we are going to discuss ways that you can start sharing that awesome personality!

The best way for your managers to know about you and your goals is for you to share that with them. The better your manager knows you, the more he or she can help you achieve your goals. You can share some general personal information, such as your hobbies and interests, but it may not serve you well to share too much of this with a boss.

However, it's important for you to share your thoughts on work-related issues so that you are on your employer's mind when there are opportunities for advancement within your company. If, for example, you express an interest in getting into management and share ideas about the contributions you could make in that role, chances are when there is an opportunity for a promotion, you will already be on the radar as a candidate.

Key questions that will inspire you to take action and create change:

1) What can you share with your managers so that they can better understand who you are and what you want to accomplish in your career?

2) Have you developed a strategy for why you want to share the things you do? How could it help you better articulate your goals?

3) What can you learn from your managers that would help you in your career? How did they get to their place in their career?

It may also be a good idea for you to get to know your managers. Ask them questions about how they got into their role. You will find that most people get excited about talking about their successes and how they've accomplished what they have. Your goal is to create an open dialogue with your managers so they see you as an equal and someone who is promotable and worthy of an investment.

CHAPTER 13

Suggest growth opportunities for your role and the business.

Leaders become leaders because they do something to earn that role. What are you contributing at your workplace to earn the status of a leader?

Just because you are not the boss yet does not mean you cannot contribute and suggest new growth opportunities for yourself and your business.

It is very common for people to complain about their positions and their employers. When I hear those complaints, I ask what they are contributing to create change. Most of the time, I hear excuses instead of constructive ideas on how people can add something to benefit their companies and themselves.

It is your job to create opportunities for yourself. Start thinking about what ideas you can contribute to benefit your company. If you have special skills that will allow you to increase your role, it is your obligation to let your employer know.

Key questions that will inspire you to take action and create change:

1) What do you think needs to change at your workplace? Are there positive ideas you can suggest?

2) Can you learn about trends in your industry that you can bring to your employer?

3) What opportunities do you see for your own growth at work?

4) Are there promotional opportunities to pursue that align with your expertise and can enrich your work experience?

Your employer will notice those who bring fresh and relevant ideas to the workplace. If you see opportunity for improvement, you have the power to share your thoughts and create change.

You also have the chance to change your trajectory at work and have input in creating compelling opportunities for your future growth.

CHAPTER 14

Don't get complacent.

Understand how to constantly advance and evolve your role. Once you see how effective you can be in the workplace, you will notice a pattern to how you can advance your career. There is a formula to success. It usually does not happen by accident.

You will start to notice a rhythm to your work flow and success. The important element to understand is that once you accomplish something at work, that is just the beginning. One-hit wonders usually don't have lasting success. You need to constantly push yourself, reinvent your image, and constantly create compelling career opportunities.

If you have completed the earlier steps in this book, you know what is important to your employer and what it needs in the workplace. If you apply that information to your efforts, you will be able to grow and evolve your role at work.

Key questions that will inspire you to take action and create change:

1) What meaningful contributions can you offer that would show your usefulness at work?

2) Do you have a big-picture, long-term strategic plan—a road map you can follow for your continued success?

3) Have you gotten complacent in your role?

4) What can you do to energize yourself, renew your purpose at work, and create change?

Again, realize that accomplishing a goal is only the beginning. You need to continue to push yourself and create a pattern of success. You will accomplish bigger and bigger goals and will realize how easy it becomes to perform at a higher level than you ever imagined.

CHAPTER 15

Elevate those around you—this also elevates your role.

I have focused this book on what you can do to increase your chances for success and earn more money, but it is also important to help elevate those around you.

There is a dual benefit to this. First, you will be helping other people accomplish their goals. When you look at your coworkers as collaborators and allies instead of competition, everyone benefits from additional opportunities.

The second benefit to helping others is that it establishes your role as a leader. Employers want their people to help one another. This kind of teamwork creates a healthy and productive environment that usually benefits the bottom line.

Key questions that will inspire you to take action and create change:

1) What can you do to help others in your workplace?

2) Are there constructive ideas you can share with others that would benefit them?

3) How can you benefit from the process of helping your peers?

4) What ideas can you bring to management that would help spotlight your role as a leader in your workplace?

You will also notice that when you are helping others, you will learn from those experiences. I always gain additional perspective when I am training or coaching others. During the process of sharing ideas, I get a better understanding of the information. It also gives us the advantage of seeing situations from many different angles.

CHAPTER 16

Do you have a job, or do you have a career?

I don't like to use the word "job" when I work with my clients. I do not "find jobs." I strategically build careers. There is a big difference.

If you look at the work you do as a job, it will be just a job. A job is a short-term task. A job is not substantial. Anyone can get a job! You want to build a career. You need to strategically plan to build a career. There is a future in a career. There is more substance and more rewards in a career.

If you consider your employment a job instead of a career, you need to figure out whether that is the case because of the limits of your role or because of you and the limited resources you apply to your work. If you are in a dead-end job, it is your responsibility to create your road map for building a substantial career. If you have a job because of your own lack of effort, start applying yourself to build your current work into a career.

As you may suspect, careers usually pay more than jobs because there are more qualifications and skills needed to obtain a career position. It is time for you to be honest with yourself and figure out how you want to spend your working hours, which, in turn, determines how you are able to spend your free time. More money equals more choices and possibly greater opportunities.

Key questions that will inspire you to take action and create change:

1) Are you stuck in a job that leaves you feeling unsatisfied and unfilled?

2) If so, why are you still in that position?

3) Are you working a job but your colleagues are building careers after starting from the same position?

4) If so, what did your peers do to build their careers that you have not done? If you cannot answer this question, you should ask those who have earned promotions.

There is absolutely nothing wrong with working a job—unless you want more out of your professional life. There are countless fantastic careers waiting for the next generation of talented stars. It is up to you to determine whether you want to reap the professional and personal rewards of stepping up, committing, and developing your career.

CHAPTER 17

Develop a strategy and a blueprint for your career.

I f you traveled to a new city and had to drive to an important meeting across town, would you just guess how to get there and drive aimlessly with no indication of where you were going? Probably not. You would most likely use a GPS or a map and determine the most efficient route to your goal.

Often, people forget to use a map for their careers, and they just aimlessly bounce around from one job to another. For you to accomplish significant goals, you need to first understand what they are and then map out the path you will take to get there. Most great successes don't happen by accident. People accomplish great things by developing realistic blueprints and taking each step necessary to accomplish their goals.

That is now your challenge—to figure out the blueprint for your career.

Key questions that will inspire you to take action and create change:

1) Can you list three to five elements of a career you would want to have? For example, what type of industry interests you? What type of work would you like to do? What salary would you like to earn?

2) What do you have to do to accomplish your above answers and goals?

3) Is there anything stopping you from accomplishing these career goals? For example, do you lack education or experience?

4) If so, what do you have to do to overcome those elements?

Now that you have developed an outline of what you really want to do, research the next steps to transform working a job into building a career.

There is nothing you can't accomplish if you devise the right strategy to guide yourself through each step. Some of the most successful people in the world have had the greatest odds against them, so if you are trying to find an excuse for why you cannot pursue and accomplish your career dreams, you are simply creating reasons for not being successful. I always look for the reasons that I *will* be a success.

CHAPTER 18

Earn a raise by selling more and earning more.

Are you working in a position or field where your efforts and talent can impact your salary? If you have a commission or bonus-type payment structure, your raise is just waiting for you to earn it.

The beauty of sales positions is their nearly unlimited earning opportunity. Just as in most professions, only a very small percentage of salespeople are truly stars. It is up to you to prove your worth and rise above average.

There are salespeople who are earning millions of dollars per year because they understand their product and their clients and know how to show the value of what they are selling.

If you are a salesperson who complains about how little you earn, you are really complaining about your own abilities.

It is time to take responsibility for your career and earn a raise by increasing your productivity.

Key questions that will inspire you to take action and create change:

1) What is the real monetary ceiling in your position? What are the top earners in similar positions making in your company?

2) Why aren't you earning more than they are?

3) What are they doing that you are not?

4) Would you be better suited to selling a different product or service or working in a different industry?

This last question is a very important one. You simply may be at the wrong company, selling the wrong product. Figure out what you love, and then find a position that matches your interest and passion. If you love what you are doing, your days will be much more interesting and rewarding. If you dread your work, you will have trouble selling because your prospective clients will know you don't believe in your offerings.

Salespeople have a high level of control over their earning potential. If you want a raise, develop a plan to increase your coverage and thereby increase your sales and your earning potential.

CHAPTER 19

Shadow a higher-ranking coworker.

Is there someone at work who has a position you would like to have someday? That person has all the answers to how you can work your way to that position and pay scale. Most people will be willing to help you if you ask.

You should figure out what position you want in your company and whom you respect and admire in that position. You could let that person know you are interested in future promotion opportunities and are interested in learning more about what he or she does in the role.

This would be a great chance for you to have a sneak peek and learn more about whether this is the career path you want to pursue. Shadowing this person will also give you valuable exposure with managers and show them you are interested in future career-advancement opportunities.

Key questions that will inspire you to take action and create change:

1) What position do you want at your workplace? Identify the person you think is a top performer in that position, and ask whether you can shadow her or him.

2) What do you want to accomplish from shadowing this person? Do you want to learn more about the position? Do you want to learn what you need to do to get to this position?

3) Do you know the good and the bad about the position? Ask the person you are shadowing about the positives and challenges of this position.

4) Is your personality a fit for this position?

5) What do you have to do to strategically chart your path to earn a possible promotion to this position?

Shadowing someone in a higher-level position is a great opportunity for you to get a general sense of what you may want to work to accomplish. It will also give you a glance at the types of skills you will need to excel in the position.

However, while shadowing, you may also discover that this is not the position you really want. This could save you some time, and you can start planning for a position that may be a better fit for your personality and goals.

CHAPTER 20

Find a mentor who is doing what you want to do.

Working with a mentor is a more in-depth process than shadowing someone, as covered in the previous chapter. A mentor relationship requires more commitment on your part, and more important, you need to find someone who is willing to take you on as a protégé.

Search for someone who has considerable experience doing what you want to do. You will quickly realize that it can be a bit tough to find someone who has not only the position you eventually want to earn but also the experience you respect and the right skills to coach you so that you gain valuable experience from the mentorship.

Key questions that will inspire you to take action and create change:

1) What specific qualities are you looking for in a mentor? Someone who works a certain position? Someone who works in a certain industry or company? Someone who is patient and has the time to mentor you?

2) What can you gain from finding the right mentor?

3) What are the specific goals you want to accomplish with your mentor?

4) What are you going to bring to the partnership so that the experience is equally beneficial to both parties? Are there skills you can bring that would help your mentor?

Successful outcomes of your mentorship ultimately depend on how selective you are in finding the right person as your mentor. That person could help guide your career for years and be instrumental in helping you identify and seize compelling career opportunities that could lead to both satisfaction and financial rewards for you.

As with most partnerships, what you get out of a mentor relationship depends on what you put into it. Your mentor will be more motivated to help and guide you if this person sees that you are a hard worker who is truly hungry for success.

CHAPTER 21

Stop being a follower. It's time to lead.

Most workplaces have a large percentage of people who are very content to be part of the herd and follow someone else's lead. These are usually the same people who complain about their lack of opportunities and pay. You can probably list the names of your coworkers who are in this category. Let's make sure you are not on the list with them.

Leaders rise to the top! Leaders command the highest salaries. Leaders earn the best opportunities. It is time that you realize your full potential and separate yourself from the pack.

It is very easy to be a follower. Someone else tells you what to do, or you simply follow by example. Being a follower does not require a lot of thinking or ingenuity. On the other hand, being a leader takes drive, initiative, and the ability to push yourself past your comfort zone.

When was the last time you did something at work to establish yourself as a leader? If you can't list specific examples, it is time for you to start changing the course of you career. Find ways that you can constructively contribute to your work team and offer something extra. Think of ways through which you can benefit the bottom line, and create initiatives to encourage growth at your workplace.

Key questions that will inspire you to take action and create change:

1) Can you define the follower mentality at your workplace? By identifying the problem, you can make sure that you don't fall into the follower category.

2) What are specific, actionable items you can implement that would elevate your status as a leader at work?

3) What have others done at your workplace that helped people recognize them as leaders?

4)   What is stopping you from taking action right now?

Growing into a leader challenges you to consistently push yourself and others to grow. To become a leader, you need to step outside of your comfort zone and do everything you can to show you are not part of the pack of followers.

Becoming a leader does not happen overnight. You need to prove yourself over time and show you have the insight, foresight, and perseverance to lead. Once you establish yourself as a leader, your skill set will be in demand, and you will be highly compensated for your expertise.

CHAPTER 22

Share your skills.

Now that we have discussed the difference between leaders and followers, there are specific actions you can take to set yourself apart from the crowd.

Do you have specialized skills that can establish you as an expert in a certain area? If so, you can leverage them to further your career. Make sure that your management knows about it. If you have a special skill set or expertise, offer to share it with your team during an informal presentation. This will set you apart as a leader.

There are many ways you can help others with your knowledge. You can offer one-on-one help, or you can offer to host informal presentations or workshops for your team members. You will want to coordinate this type of activity with your manager to make sure he or she wants you to contribute in this way and that it would offer value to your coworkers.

Key questions that will inspire you to take action and create change:

1) What unique and useful expertise do you have that you can share with your coworkers?

2) How can you demonstrate to your manager that your presentation of information would benefit your coworkers?

3) Can you identity additional training information that you can keep presenting to your coworkers on a continual basis? You could ask your manager to send you to seminars or conventions where you can gain additional knowledge, then agree to share that information with your coworkers.

4) Can you develop additional supporting materials that would continue to advance the information you present to the group? This will help others at your work

further apply the information you share with them at your presentations.

If you are able to present information to others at work, you will earn a reputation for being an expert. This will prove your value to your management and show that you bring innovative ideas and are also willing to share them with others.

You will also find that you learn while teaching others. This continues to contribute to your knowledge base and solidify your status as an expert.

CHAPTER 23

Understand your value in the marketplace.

One of the best ways to earn what you are worth is to know what you are worth. When you buy a house, you generally get an appraisal for the property. You should use the same care in evaluating your own worth in the marketplace—get your own "appraisal."

The best way to determine how much money you could earn is to launch a career search. In my business, after we conduct a thorough search for our clients, we have a very accurate idea of how much money they can command in the workplace. Once you understand your value, then you have the data you need to get the salary you want.

Key questions that will inspire you to take action and create change:

1) After you conduct a thorough career search, what is the financial range of offers you receive?

2) Are there salary differences based on location? Be sure to account for cost-of-living differences when estimating your worth. For example, the same salary will go a lot further in a city with a low cost of living than it would in an expensive city like San Francisco.

3) Do you notice a trend in the salary range of offers you see in your career search?

Normally, most offers fall into a similar salary range, with a few below and sometimes a few higher than the others. If you keep accurate notes and track the trends, you will get an honest assessment of how much money you could potentially earn.

With this salary figure, you can prove to your current or potential employer that your earning potential is higher than what you are currently earning. Don't expect this to equate to an instant raise, but it is more leverage for you to negotiate a salary more commensurate with your current skill set and talent.

CHAPTER 24

Understand the value of your position and title.

Now that you have an accurate appraisal of your potential value, you should understand why it is important that you earn what you are really worth. Throughout this book, I have pointed out that people often complain about their salaries but do nothing to change their situations and earn more money.

That is why it is your responsibility to know how much you should really be getting paid and how one earns that level of salary. The problem I often see is that when people accept new positions at below-market value, most of the time, they continue to be underpaid throughout their entire employment at that company.

Most companies base raises on your current salary. If you start at a new company earning a below-market salary, management often has a tough time justifying a huge raise to put you on par with the going rate for your position any time in the future. This means that when you start a new position, you need to do your research and figure out what the salary market range is for your position and command money in that range.

I tell my clients the most important number when you are starting a new position is your first-year salary. It truly dictates your future earning power at that company.

Key questions that will inspire you to take action and create change:

1) Do you know what the salary range is for your position?

2) Can you offer data to your employer that shows why this position should pay a certain amount? Most industries have salary studies that you can readily find on the Internet.

3) Are you prepared to turn down an offer of employment if the salary is not in line with what it should be?

4) Can you negotiate a higher salary? Once you know
what is important to prospective employers, you can
address their needs with your talents and try to sell
your case—why you are worth every penny!

As you develop your career strategy, you will find that real
data and analytics are key to navigating your career. Without
accurate and relevant information, you are doing yourself and
your employer a major disservice. Understanding the facts
will help you accomplish your goals and strategically map out
the path to your ultimate success.

CHAPTER 25

Express opinions about work
strategically.

Sometimes the most vocal people at work get a majority of the attention and the rewards. Those who speak up and have substance in their messages gain recognition over coworkers who do not contribute as much.

If your workplace culture encourages your feedback and participation, you should really take advantage of those opportunities. In addition to demonstrating to management that you are promotable and deserving of raises, you are also contributing to make your workplace a more positive and productive environment.

Just make sure you know your role in your workplace and understand how much flexibility you have to share your thoughts. Of course, many people get passionate when they share their ideas and want to create change. If other people express significant resistance to some of your ideas, make sure you are open to other people's thoughts, and be flexible with your direction. It's great to share your ideas, but never be combative if you meet resistance when presenting your thoughts.

Key questions that will inspire you to take action and create change:

1) What ways can you contribute and share ideas that will have a positive impact on your workplace?

2) Are there certain things you think your company could be doing better?

3) What are your biggest obstacles to being successful at work? Can you suggest alternatives that may help you and your coworkers overcome those obstacles?

4) Are you presenting your ideas in a positive and constructive tone?

Nobody likes a bully. Make sure that you are respectful of the process that your company has established for you to share your feedback. Many times, the way you present your ideas is just as important as the ideas themselves. The more people like you, the more they will support you in accomplishing your goals.

CHAPTER 26

Give management feedback about your role, and express how you could further enhance the company's mission.

Do you feel like there are elements of your position that are wasting the company's resources? Could your role be reshaped to be more effective and beneficial to the company? Often the person who knows most about your position is you!

Because of changes at your company or an evolving industry, the purpose of your position will also need to evolve. If you feel there are parts of your role that are antiquated, you should share that with your management.

Some people are reluctant to share that information with management for fear that their roles may be eliminated. While there is a small chance of that happening, I think there is a greater chance of your management being impressed that you are stepping forward and sharing your thoughts on how you could modify your role to increase your productivity.

Key questions that will inspire you to take action and create change:

1) Are there tasks you perform that seem unnecessary?

2) Are there other functions that should be part of your role but are currently not?

3) Are there parts of your position that are redundant or that overlap with your coworkers' responsibilities?

4) Can you offer constructive feedback that would evolve your role and be beneficial to your company?

As you help rewrite your role at your company, you are demonstrating that you are a valuable member of the team who really does care about the overall well-being of the organization.

There is also the possibility that by you adding new responsibilities, you will be rewarded with a raise and future growth opportunities.

CHAPTER 27

Find a new position.

Sometimes getting a raise from your current employer is impossible. If earning more money is high on your priority list, you may need to change companies.

I find that people get the biggest raises when they get a position at a new company. That truly is the best time for you to negotiate your highest salary. If you have relevant skills, you may find that your talents are in high demand at your employer's competitors, who may be willing to pay top dollar for your expertise.

Changing companies is also a great time to earn a promotion you may want. Your goal at a new company should be to accomplish all the items you feel like you are not able to at your current employer. Once you are able to identify what you want, then you can start developing your strategy to get it.

Key questions that will inspire you to take action and create change:

1) Are there other companies in your industry that offer additional elements of the compensation package that you would prefer but may not be getting now?

2) Who is the leader in your industry? There are many benefits to working for an innovative company that is known as one of the best employers in your field.

3) What in-demand skills do you possess that could earn you top dollar?

4) What accomplishments have you achieved that would make you a marketable asset to prospective employers?

If you find that your current position and company are dead ends in your career, there is little incentive on your part to invest more of your valuable time and expertise in a situation that is not right for you. Just make sure that your expectations are realistic when you create your wish list of what you want from your next position. Remember, in most cases, you will get the largest raise when you switch companies. You just have to make sure that the grass really is greener on the other side and that you will be happy working at a new company.

CHAPTER 28

Don't disclose your current salary to potential employers.

One of the most common questions many prospective employers ask potential employees is how much they currently make. I advise you not to share that with a prospective employer.

Prospective employers ask the question for many reasons. First, they may just want to make sure that their current opening is a fit for the salary range you want to earn. Most hiring managers are busy and don't have the time to interview people if the salary range is not a fit for a candidate. Why waste the time interviewing if the salary range is way below your requirements? I certainly respect that idea of not wasting time. There are, however, more constructive ways to figure out if the employer and the employee are a good match in the salary range. Either side could simply mention a general range to determine if both parties have similar goals for salary.

Some employers ask your current salary simply to see if they can give you the smallest raise you will accept. I do not think this is fair, as what you *earn* now is not necessarily reflective of what you are *worth* now.

I suggest you ask about the salary range for the position at an appropriate point in the interview process. If an employer asks how much money you are currently earning, you could simply say that out of respect for your current employer, you prefer not to share that information. Additionally, say that you would like your future salary to be based on your talents, skills, expertise, and potential contributions to the company.

Key questions that will inspire you to take action and create change:

1) Do you see any value in disclosing your current salary to prospective employers? If it is low or high, either could have a negative impact on what you can earn with your future employer—or even your chances of receiving an offer.

2) Can you convincingly explain why you prefer not to share your current salary?

3) Are you prepared to explain how you view your current worth, based on your valuable experience and talents?

As I write this book, many states in America have now passed legislation that prohibits employers from asking candidates their current salary. Similar legislation is currently pending in a number of other states. These laws are designed to protect applicants and allow people to earn a salary based on market value, not on what a current or previous employer pays.

CHAPTER 29

Don't bring your personal life or drama to work.

I wanted to make sure I mentioned this point. Some people automatically disqualify themselves for raises because they prove through repeated actions that they have not earned them.

It should go without saying that during work hours, you should leave your personal life outside and focus on business. I have seen so many talented people fail at this and never be considered for raises or promotions because they are distracted at work. Yes, we all have situations in our personal lives that occasionally distract us, but your employer pays you to work, so that is what you should do in return for your paycheck.

Your employers not only judge you based on your production but also look at other factors: how you relate with others in the workplace, how open you are to constructive feedback, and whether you are a person free from drama and distractions at work.

Key questions that will inspire you to take action and create change:

1) Are you bringing your personal life and problems to work?

2) Do you arrive at work ready to tackle your duties, or are you distracted by your personal issues?

3) What is your reputation at work? Are you known as a productive contributor or as someone who is always dealing with personal problems?

4) If you realize that you are bringing your personal life to work, what immediate steps can you take to adjust this to ensure your success?

As employers evaluate top performers on the team, they often look at the entirety of someone's performance. Even if you are a hard worker, if your personal life consistently gets in the way of your work, it will probably be a roadblock to your success.

Of course, certain serious personal situations can unfortunately interfere with our ability to focus at work. Your employer should respect your need to be attentive to those matters, as long as you can distinguish the difference between a life-altering event that requires your focus and a routine tendency for you to surround yourself with chaos and drama.

CHAPTER 30

Ask for a raise.

Now that we have reviewed twenty-nine steps that will increase your chances of earning a raise, let's not forget about a very important step—ask for a raise!

You have to ask for the things you want in life. If you don't, no one will know you want them. But before you ask for a raise, make sure the time is appropriate and that you can show you have earned the right to ask for more money. Have you accomplished something spectacular that would warrant a raise?

Your employer may not take you seriously if you ask for a raise only weeks after you start a new position. So, make sure your timing is right in relation to how long you have worked in your position and the timing of the company's revenues.

If you work at a company that earns a high percentage of its revenue in a certain season or month, you may be more likely to receive a raise if you ask then.

Key questions that will inspire you to take action and create change:

1) What is the most tactful and professional way for you to ask for a raise? For example, it's probably not the best to ask via e-mail. You may come across as rude and lazy.

2) Do you have regular performance reviews? One of those could be a great time for you to introduce your proposal for a raise. If your manager does not offer performance reviews, you could suggest one.

3) What specific reasons can you present to your employer to justify your request for a raise? What have you done to increase your value at your company?

4) What is the culture for raises at your company?

It is important that you understand the protocol at your company for how people earn raises. You want to make sure you are operating in a way that your employer will respect and understand. If you come across as offensive, your efforts of asking for a raise will probably count against you.

If you truly believe you have earned a raise, you should ask for one. If you feel like you are underpaid, it is your responsibility to respectfully share with your employer why you are a great candidate for a raise.

Overall Thoughts

While the focus of this book is about how to get a raise, I want to bring up a very important point. Oftentimes, many other factors will be important to you rather than simply your salary or a raise.

While how much money you earn is important, I consider career satisfaction one of the most crucial factors to happiness. As a talent agent, I rank my success with my clients by how happy they are with the careers we build as a team.

You can earn a lot of money, but if you are absolutely miserable in your position, eventually the money will not be enough to motivate you to do well or encourage your happiness. I don't always advise my clients to accept the highest-paying offers.

There are so many other factors that could be more important. For example, what is the culture in a workplace? Are people happy and vibrant, or do they seem to be miserable and moping around?

Do you get along with and respect your prospective employers and coworkers? Are these the people you want to work with every day? What duties will you perform in your new position? Will you be satisfied and content doing these tasks after a few months? A few years? Will you feel accomplished doing this type of work?

You have to decide what factors are important to you. Some people forgo raises for other benefits, such as additional time off or flexible work schedules.

If you put the initial investment into developing your career strategy and maintaining it to make sure you are always working toward your long-term goals, along the way you will find out what is important to you and how to accomplish what you want and need to feel happy, satisfied, and successful.

About the Author

The CEO of a national broadcast talent firm, Jeff Marcu is known for his ability to double, triple, or even quadruple his clients' salaries while transforming their careers.

Marcu's transformative playbook is now available to you. In *30 Days to a Raise*, Marcu shares the powerful but simple techniques he uses to help his clients achieve their dreams.

As an acclaimed journalist with an Emmy and multiple Edward R. Murrow Awards, Marcu credits his success to the techniques he describes in *30 Days to a Raise*. After implementing these concepts in his life, Marcu has built a thriving national business, invented and successfully launched a popular consumer product, and developed a series of books. Companies and organizations frequently seek out Marcu's expertise through his transformative and interactive live presentations.

Now you have access to the same formula that can rapidly change your career and your life. By sharing the strategies he has developed throughout his career, Marcu effectively describes each step you need to take to uncover your true potential and live the life you have always wanted.